Collins

English in 5 minutes

Grammar, punctuation and spelling activities

Shelley Welsh

CONTENTS

HOW TO USE THIS BOOK

The best way to help your child to build their confidence in English grammar, punctuation and spelling is to give them lots and lots of practice in the key topics and skills.

Written by English experts, this series will help your child master English grammar, punctuation and spelling, and prepare them for SATs.

This book provides ready-to-practise questions that comprehensively cover the English grammar, punctuation and spelling curriculum for Year 6. It contains:

- 36 topic-based tests, each 5 minutes long, to help your child build up their grammar, punctuation and spelling knowledge day-by-day.

- 4 mixed topic tests (Progress Tests), each 5 minutes long, to check progress by covering a mix of topics from the previous 9 tests.

Each test is divided into three Steps:

- **Step 1: Review (1 minute)**
  This exercise helps your child to revise grammar, punctuation and spelling topics they should already know and prepares them for Step 2.

- **Step 2: Practise (2½ minutes)**
  This exercise is a set of questions focused on the topic area being tested.

- **Step 3: Challenge (1½ minutes)**
  This is a more testing exercise designed to stretch your child and deepen their understanding.

Some of the tests also include a Tip to help your child answer questions of a particular type.

Your child should attempt to answer as many questions as possible in the time allowed at each Step. Answers are provided at the back of the book.

To help to measure progress, each test includes boxes for recording the date of the test, the total score obtained, and the total time taken. One mark is awarded for each written part of the answer.

Acknowledgements

The authors and publisher are grateful to the copyright holders for permission to use quoted materials and images.

All images are © HarperCollins*Publishers* Ltd and © Shutterstock.com

Every effort has been made to trace copyright holders and obtain their permission for the use of copyright material. The authors and publisher will gladly receive information enabling them to rectify any error or omission in subsequent editions. All facts are correct at time of going to press.

Published by Collins
An imprint of HarperCollins*Publishers*
1 London Bridge Street
London SE1 9GF

HarperCollins*Publishers*
1st Floor, Watermarque Building,
Ringsend Road, Dublin 4, Ireland

ISBN: 978-0-00-844945-2

First published 2021

10 9 8 7 6 5 4 3 2 1

British Library Cataloguing in Publication Data.

A CIP record of this book is available from the British Library.

Author: Shelley Welsh
Publisher: Fiona McGlade
Project Manager: Chantal Addy
Editor: Jill Laidlaw
Cover Design: Kevin Robbins and Sarah Duxbury
Inside Concept Design: Paul Oates and Ian Wrigley
Typesetting Services: Jouve India Private Limited
Production: Karen Nulty
Printed in Great Britain by Martins the Printers

Tip *Nouns are naming words for things, people, animals and places.* **Proper nouns** *name particular people, places, days of the week, months of the year, books and films.*

STEP 1 **Review**

Tip *Adjectives provide more information about nouns and people. For example,* Billy is **tired**. *or It was an* **exceptional** *day.*

Underline the **two nouns** in each sentence below.

The children walked to school because it was warm and sunny.

There are plenty of paints in the cupboard if you look hard.

Underline the **two adjectives** in each sentence below.

When they saw the glimmering light, they were hopeful someone was in the cottage.

Arriving at our final destination, we were thrilled to find there was a funfair.

STEP 2  **Practise**

Tip *Some nouns cannot be physically seen – they are abstract. For example, Natalia has so much* **love** *for her new puppy.*

Underline the **three abstract nouns** in the passage below.

It was with great fear but considerable determination that Damian approached the huge beast; he would strike the creature with his magic sword, and then he could continue his quest.

STEP 3 (1.5 min) **Challenge**

Which sentence below is correctly punctuated?

Last May, Mr Thomas visited Madagascar in the Indian ocean. ☐

Last May, mr Thomas visited Madagascar in the Indian ocean. ☐

Last May, Mr Thomas visited madagascar in the Indian ocean. ☐

Last May, Mr Thomas visited Madagascar in the Indian Ocean. ☐

Time spent: _____ min _____ sec. Total: _____ out of 12

Date: _____

Day of week: _____

Tip *A noun phrase is a phrase where a noun is the main word, modified by another word or words. For example, new shoes / my new shoes. Noun phrases can be expanded further. For example, my new shoes with the silver logo.*

STEP 1 (1 min) Review

Add an adjective to turn each noun into a **noun phrase**.

_____ butterflies   _____ parrots

_____ monkeys   _____ stars

STEP 2 (2.5 min) Practise

Underline the longest **noun phrase** in each sentence.

Ramat and his two best friends listened eagerly to the interesting talk delivered by the explorer.

Some naughty children from Class B have dropped litter in the playground.

Florence, a talented baker, created an iced sponge cake topped with eleven candles.

The nervous thief dropped the bag containing a hoard of stolen jewellery.

STEP 3 (1.5 min) Challenge

Write a sentence containing an **expanded noun phrase**.

_____

_____

_____

Date: _____

Day of week: _____

Tip *A verb tells you what someone or something is doing, being or having.*

STEP 1 (1 min) Review

Underline the **two verbs** in each sentence below.

We packed our bags and loaded the car.

Mum used kindling to light the campfire.

Eva has a bad cold so she is going to bed early.

"I have two cats and a dog," Xavier told me.

Tip *An adverb tells you more information about a verb. An adverb can modify a verb, an adjective, another adverb or a whole clause. An adverb can tell you how, where or when something happens.*

STEP 2 (2.5 min) Practise

Which sentence contains an **adverb**?

Viktor worked hard on his times tables revision. ☐

Noor thought the maths test was hard. ☐

I banged my elbow on the hard surface. ☐

We told Ali it was hard luck that he lost his trainers. ☐

In which sentence is <u>lead</u> used as a **verb**?

I used a dark lead pencil to do my sketch. ☐

The dog's lead was caught on a branch. ☐

The teachers lead the children into the playground. ☐

STEP 3 (1.5 min) Challenge

What is the **word class** of each underlined word?

Gretchen <u>carefully</u> takes the cake out of the oven. _____

Gretchen is <u>careful</u> when she takes the cake out of the oven. _____

Gretchen takes <u>care</u> when she takes the cake out of the oven. _____

Time spent: _____ min _____ sec. Total: _____ out of 13

Date: _____

Day of week: _____

Tip *A coordinating conjunction such as 'and', 'but' and 'or' can link clauses, words or phrases as an equal pair. For example, Niamh has a dog **and** a cat.*

STEP 1 (1 min) Review

Underline a **coordinating** and a **subordinating conjunction** in each sentence below.

We packed our waterproofs and boots because rain was predicted over the weekend.

Although we don't have high-tech computers or up-to-date gym equipment, our school is amazing.

*A subordinating conjunction, such as 'although', 'as' and 'before', introduces a subordinate clause; a subordinate clause is dependent on a main clause, otherwise it doesn't make sense. For example, We were tired **because we ran all the way home**. The words in bold are a subordinate clause, dependent on the main clause 'We were tired'.*

STEP 2 (2.5 min) Practise

Tick **one** box in each row to show whether the underlined words are a **main clause** or a **subordinate clause**.

Sentence	Main clause	Subordinate clause
We watched the new Harry Potter film <u>after we celebrated Dad's birthday</u>.		
As neither of us were wearing a watch, <u>Vim and I missed the last bus</u>.		
Although my alarm clock hadn't yet gone off, <u>I got up</u>.		
The children took shelter under a large oak tree <u>so that they wouldn't get wet</u>.		

Tip *When the sentence starts with the subordinate clause, it is followed by a comma.*

STEP 3 (1.5 min) Challenge

Insert a **subordinating conjunction** to show that Millie's gran cooks and listens to the radio at the same time.

Millie's gran cooks _____ she listens to the radio.

Rewrite the sentence below so that it starts with the **subordinate clause**.

Sarah ran back to the house when she realised she had forgotten her homework.

_____

5 Relative clauses

Date: _____

Day of week: _____

Tip A **relative clause** is a type of subordinate clause, introduced by a **relative pronoun** which gives more information about the preceding noun. The relative pronouns are: **who, which, that, whose, where, when, whom.** For example, *I'm friends with Ginny, who lives next door.*

STEP 1 (1 min) **Review**

 Tip *Sometimes the relative pronoun can be left out.*

Tick **one** box in each row to show whether the underlined words are a **main clause** or a **relative clause**.

Sentence	Main clause	Relative clause
<u>We played the game</u> which you bought us for Christmas.		
Our Irish cousins, <u>with whom we are going on holiday,</u> are great fun.		
<u>There's the man</u> whose house burnt down last month.		
The musical <u>I wanted to see</u> has sold out.		

STEP 2 (2.5 min) **Practise**

Insert a **relative pronoun** to complete each sentence below.

The caretaker, _____ shed is in the playground, was annoyed to find it had been vandalised.

Mrs Kamal, _____ is my teacher, is very kind and patient.

The hospital _____ Dad was born is now derelict.

"To _____ does this book belong?" asked our teacher.

STEP 3 (1.5 min) **Challenge**

 Tip *Sometimes, the relative pronoun can refer back to the whole clause that comes before it. For example, Our kettle has broken, which means Mum can't have a cup of tea.*

Complete the sentences below with a suitable **relative clause**.

Maria, _____, speaks Spanish.

The book _____ was brilliant.

Our new car keeps breaking down, _____.

Time spent: _____ min _____ sec. Total: _____ out of 11

Date: _____

Day of week: _____

STEP 1 (1 min) Review

Underline the **pronoun** in each sentence below.

We are going fishing in the morning.

I have cereal for breakfast every morning.

"Do you cycle to school or take the bus?"

The weather forecaster said it would snow later.

STEP 2 (2.5 min) Practise

Replace the underlined words with a suitable **pronoun**.

Fergus enjoys playing tennis but <u>Fergus</u> _____ isn't very keen on golf.

Both children studied hard for the test and <u>the children</u> _____ got top marks.

Mum and I went shopping and <u>Mum and I</u> _____ bought new shoes.

I have broken my computer; my friend Jim is coming to fix <u>my computer</u> _____.

STEP 3 (1.5 min) Challenge

Complete each sentence with a suitable **pronoun**.

The boys ran towards their dad, full of joy at seeing _____ after so long.

Mum brought Aisling and _____ some toast for our supper.

We had a lesson on rivers; _____ was very interesting to learn about their journey.

Fred told _____ that she should listen more carefully in class.

The teacher gave Ronil and _____ some extra paper.

"Sal and _____ are heading to the park," I informed Mum.

Date: _____

Day of week: _____

 Tip *A **possessive pronoun** shows ownership of a noun. It replaces a noun to avoid repetition and shows possession. For example, This is my hat; **yours** is over there. 'yours' replaces 'your hat'.*

STEP 1 (1 min) Review

Underline the **possessive pronoun** in each sentence.

These are my books but I've no idea where yours are.

I've given them my suggestions for a new game but they haven't given me theirs.

Tom has found his bike but I can't find mine anywhere.

If I tell you my phone number, will you please let me have yours so I can send you a text?

STEP 2 (2.5 min) Practise

Write each underlined word in the correct column below.

I have made a cake for you. I hope you like it.

We have brought our football but we can see you've not brought yours.

Ours is the best model out of them all but theirs is almost as good.

Have you seen Lili's book? She thinks she gave it to him but he says it's his.

Pronouns	Possessive pronouns

STEP 3 (1.5 min) Challenge

Replace the underlined words with the correct **pronoun**.

With no time to lose, Joe raced towards the finish line. Joe briefly glanced over his

[ ]

shoulder; Grace was closing in on Joe and Grace didn't seem tired, so Joe knew he

[ ] [ ] [ ]

had to put some distance between him and Grace.

[ ]

Time spent: _____ min _____ sec. Total: _____ out of 21

> **Tip**
> A **preposition** links a noun, pronoun or noun phrase to another word in the sentence.
> It can tell you where something is in relation to something else in the sentence.
> For example, The dish is **on** the table. A preposition can also show direction and time.
> For example, The plane taxied **towards** the runway and departed **at** 4:15pm.

STEP 1 (1 min) Review

Underline the **preposition** in each sentence below.

We walked across the field.

The computer sits on the office desk.

Our cat sleeps in a basket.

There are crumbs under the kitchen table.

STEP 2 (2.5 min) Practise

Complete each sentence with a suitable **preposition**.

Mum drove _____ the roundabout until she found the right exit.

The balloon sailed _____ the air above us.

Ciara tiptoed _____ the sleeping baby.

Dad wrote his signature _____ the bottom of the form.

Naomi met Euan _____ six o'clock.

STEP 3 (1.5 min) Challenge

Circle the **four prepositions** in the sentence below.

The spider crawled along the window sill, up the curtain and back to its web in the corner.

Which sentence does **not** contain a **preposition**?

The criminal was asked to stand before the court. ☐

Before we leave home, we usually activate the alarm. ☐

My dog stood before me, a large stick in his mouth. ☐

9 Determiners

> **Tip** *A determiner can be used for a specific (known) noun, or a non-specific (unknown) noun. For example, **The** pencil over there is mine. I gave Elaya **a** pencil. Other determiners include: this, that, these, those, some, every.*

STEP 1 (1 min) Review

Underline the **two determiners** in each sentence.

We watched a policeman chase two criminals.

We ate some fruit after we had finished the pizza.

I think this book is better than that one.

These chocolate biscuits are better than those coconut creams.

STEP 2 (2.5 min) Practise

> **Tip** *A **possessive determiner** shows ownership of the following noun. For example, We saw **your** new dog earlier.*

Circle **two possessive determiners** in each sentence below.

My dad kindly said I could borrow his computer as mine is broken.

Wendy took a photo of her dog and sent it to my big brother.

Your new coat suits you and I like your matching scarf.

"Do you want sauce on your chips?" Ben asked his younger brother.

STEP 3 (1.5 min) Challenge

Complete each sentence with suitable **determiners**.

I have _____ felt pens and _____ colouring pencils.

At the zoo, we saw _____ elephant and _____ orangutan.

Gabby slipped on _____ wet moss and hurt _____ knee.

There are _____ reasons why I don't like sprouts and _____ smell is just one!

Time spent: _____ min _____ sec. Total: _____ out of 24   ©HarperCollins*Publishers* 2021

Date: _____

Day of Week: _____

STEP 1 (1 min) Review

- Add a suitable **adverb** to the sentence below.

  The dogs ran _____ towards the river.

- Rewrite the sentence below using the correct punctuation.

  the river thames runs through london and is 215 miles long

  _____

- What is the grammatical term for the underlined words?

  Harvey neatly stacked <u>the new, lined exercise books </u>on the shelf.

  _____

STEP 2 (2.5 min) Practise

- Underline the **two prepositions** in the sentence below.

  The divers swam through an underwater cave and emerged on the other side.

- Tick the **word class** the underlined words belong to.

  I received <u>an</u> award for <u>my</u> art project.

  pronouns ☐   determiners ☐   prepositions ☐   possessive pronouns ☐

- What type of clause is underlined in the sentence?

  The storm, <u>which was predicted</u>, was not as bad as anticipated. _____

- What is the grammatical term for the underlined word?

  I've seen your new puppy but you haven't seen <u>ours</u>. _____

STEP 3 (1.5 min) Challenge

- What **word class** do the underlined words belong to?

  <u>When</u> you have finished, you can go outside to play.

  We are allowed to stay up late <u>if </u>there is a film on. _____

- Complete the sentence with a **possessive determiner**.

  Floyd approached the gaping mouth of the cave; he stopped abruptly and considered _____ options.

- What is the **word class** of each underlined word?

  Matty's scarf <u>matches</u> his hat. _____

  Matty's scarf is a close <u>match</u> to his hat. _____

Tip *The* **subject** *of a sentence is the noun, noun phrase, pronoun or proper noun that is performing the action. Look for the* **verb** *to help you find the* **subject**.

STEP 1 (1 min) Review

Underline the **subject** of each sentence below.

Sheena dropped the vase on the floor.

The park keeper worked hard to fix the broken slide.

They found a ten-pound note behind the shed.

Huge waves crashed onto the jagged rocks.

Tip *The* **object** *is the noun, noun phrase, pronoun or proper noun that comes* **after the verb** *and shows what the verb is 'acting on'.*

STEP 2 (2.5 min) Practise

Circle the **object** in each sentence below.

"Will you please pass the pepper?"

Seb planted the seeds in the soil.

We drove the car to the seaside.

They encountered a long queue at the airport.

STEP 3 (1.5 min) Challenge

Label each box with **S** for **subject** or **O** for **object**.

"Will the boys come to the staffroom at lunchtime, please?" announced the teacher.
☐ ☐

Ethan bought a blue hat with his pocket money and he gave it to his brother.
☐ ☐ ☐ ☐

Time spent: _____ min _____ sec. Total: _____ out of 14

Tip | *A **statement** is a sentence that gives information about something. It starts with a capital letter and ends with a full stop. A **question** asks something. It starts with a capital letter and ends with a question mark.*

STEP 1 (1 min) Review

Tick the sentence that must end with a **question mark**.

What an exciting adventure you've had ☐

What was the result of your maths test ☐

When we get home, we will phone Grandma ☐

How fabulous it must be to live by the sea ☐

Write a **statement** you could make to tell someone **three** facts about yourself.

_____

_____

STEP 2 (2.5 min) Practise

Turn the following statement into a **question**. Do not use any additional words.

Ben has finished his homework on time this week.

_____

Write a **question** to go with this answer.

Question:_____

Answer: We have two dogs and three cats.

STEP 3 (1.5 min) Challenge

Write a **question** you would ask your favourite celebrity if you wanted to know what inspired them.

_____

_____

Tip *A **command sentence** contains a command verb. It starts with a capital letter and can end with a full stop or an exclamation mark.*

STEP 1 (1 min) Review

Which sentence below is a **command**?

You must be freezing cold in such a thin T-shirt. ☐

There can't possibly be any more rain. ☐

Please bring your PE kit to school tomorrow. ☐

When you've read the book, you must return it. ☐

Write a **command** that you would say if you wanted help to lift a heavy weight.

_____

STEP 2 (2.5 min) Practise

Underline the **two** words that show the sentence below is a **command**.

Switch on your tablet and press the link to the wildlife website.

Which sentence below is an **exclamation sentence**?

Stop making so much noise! ☐

What a lot of noise you're making! ☐

There's no point shouting at me! ☐

I heard you the first time! ☐

Tip
*An **exclamation sentence** starts with 'How...' or 'What...', contains a verb and ends with an exclamation mark.*

Write an **exclamation sentence** you might say if you received a surprise present.

_____

STEP 3 (1.5 min) Challenge

Which sentence must **not** end with an **exclamation mark**?

How shocking the news was this morning ☐

Come down here right now, please ☐

When will you have completed the jigsaw ☐

Prove to me that you are not the thief ☐

Time spent: _____ min _____ sec. Total: _____ out of 7

©HarperCollins*Publishers* 2021

Date: _____

Day of week: _____

> **Tip** The **simple present tense** is formed from the basic form of the verb (the infinitive). For example, the verb 'think' → I think, she thinks.

STEP 1 (1 min) Review

Which sentence uses **tense** correctly?

The performers take position on stage and waited for the music to start. ☐

The performers took position on stage and wait for the music to start. ☐

The performers take position on stage and were waiting for the music to start. ☐

The performers take position on stage and wait for the music to start. ☐

Complete the sentence below with a suitable **verb** in the correct **tense**.

Zac painted a picture and _____ it to his mum.

> **Tip** The **simple past tense** is formed from the basic form of the verb (the infinitive). For example, the verb 'buy' → I bought, he bought.

STEP 2 (2.5 min) Practise

Complete the passage so that it is in the correct **tense**. Use the verbs in the brackets.

After the long hike this morning, I _____ (lie) down for a rest. When I got my

breath back, I _____ (eat) a bowl of pasta. It's amazing how a meal full of

carbohydrates _____ (recharge) your batteries! I _____ (feel) on

top of the world now and ready to face the rest of the day.

STEP 3 (1.5 min) Challenge

Rewrite the underlined **simple past tense** verbs so that they are in the **simple present tense**.

The explorers greeted the villagers and were delighted with their warm welcome. Their

[_____]   [_____]

hosts invited them to attend a celebration meal, which they gratefully accepted.

[_____]   [_____]

While they waited for the preparations to be completed, they pitched their tents and

[_____]   [_____]

freshened up.

[_____]

Date: _____

Day of week: _____

> **Tip** The **present perfect tense** is formed from the present tense of the verb 'have' and the past participle of the main verb. For example, She **has eaten** her breakfast.

STEP 1 ⏱(1 min) Review

Which option correctly completes the sentence so that it is in the **present perfect** tense?

Recently there _____ some torrential rainstorms, resulting in flooding in many areas.

are being ☐   have been ☐

had been ☐   are ☐

Complete the sentence below with a suitable **verb** so that it is in the **present perfect** tense.

Enda _____ his homework at long last!

> **Tip** The **past perfect tense** is formed from the past tense of the verb 'have' and the past participle of the main verb. For example, She **had eaten** her breakfast.

STEP 2 ⏱(2.5 min) Practise

Rewrite the underlined verbs so that they are in the **past perfect** tense.

Although I <u>tried</u> many times to phone Mr Abernethy, there <u>was</u> no reply. Without

[_____]   [_____]

doubt, he <u>ignored</u> all my calls, as I <u>saw</u> him leave his office one day, indicating that he

[_____]   [_____]

was clearly still in London.

STEP 3 ⏱(1.5 min) Challenge

Which sentence is closest in meaning to the one below?

Our grandparents have had a caravan for five years.

Our grandparents are going to get a caravan. ☐

Our grandparents have a caravan now. ☐

Our grandparents will buy a caravan in five years. ☐

Our grandparents had a caravan in the past but no longer. ☐

_____

Date: _____

Day of week: _____

Tip The **present progressive tense** shows an action that is continuing to happen. It is formed from the present tense of the verb 'to be' and the present participle of the main verb. For example, The birds **are singing** in the trees.

STEP 1 (1 min) Review

Which sentence shows a **continuous action** in the present tense?

Mum was hanging up the picture. ☐

Mum is hanging up the picture. ☐

Mum has hung up the picture. ☐

Mum hung up the picture. ☐

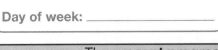

Complete the sentence with a suitable verb to show a **continuous action** in the present tense.

The teachers _____ the visitors around the school.

STEP 2 (2.5 min) Practise

Underline the **four** verbs that are in the **present progressive** tense.

We are helping Dad clear the garden shed. He asked us ages ago but we have always made excuses! We are throwing all the junk into a skip while Dad is tidying his tools. He is being particularly fussy about keeping the ones that had belonged to his grandfather.

STEP 3 (1.5 min) Challenge

Tick the box in each row to show whether each sentence is in the **simple present**, **simple past** or **present progressive** tense.

Sentence	Simple present	Simple past	Present progressive
The geese are migrating from Iceland towards the east coast of Scotland.			
We watch them through our binoculars.			
Last year, they arrived in early September.			

Date: _____

Day of week: _____

Tip The **past progressive tense** shows a continuous action in the past. It is formed from the past tense of the verb 'to be' and the present participle of the main verb. For example, *The birds* **were singing** *in the trees.*

STEP 1 (1 min) Review

Tick **one** box in each row to show whether the sentences are in the **present progressive** or **past progressive** tense.

Sentence	Present progressive	Past progressive
The royal family is gathering on the balcony to greet the crowd.		
Jaime was being unkind to his sister at breakfast.		
I'm having some friends round for pizza tonight.		

STEP 2 (2.5 min) Practise

Complete the sentences using the **past progressive** form of the verbs in the brackets.

As Dad _____ (go) to work, he met our neighbour Mrs Stewart. She

_____ (stand) at the bus stop and as it _____ (rain), Dad

offered her a lift. She refused as she _____ (meet) a friend on the bus.

Write a sentence in the **past progressive** tense about something you were doing yesterday.

_____

STEP 3 (1.5 min) Challenge

Which sentence is in the **past progressive** tense?

As usual, we were late for school.   ☐

We were waiting ages for the train.   ☐

It's been late for the last few days.   ☐

I'm definitely complaining about it.   ☐

Rewrite the following sentence in the **past progressive tense**.

Meg went to the gym to search for her missing PE kit.

_____

Write a sentence in the **past progressive tense** using the verb 'to learn'.

_____

Time spent: _____ min _____ sec. Total: _____ out of 11   ©HarperCollins*Publishers* 2021

Date: _____

Day of week: _____

Tip *Modal verbs* can show degrees of certainty, ability and obligation.

STEP 1 (1 min) Review

Circle the **modal verb** in each sentence of the passage below.

The head teacher has said we can have a non-uniform day on Friday. However, we must make a contribution to the charity we are supporting. I asked if I could bring in some cakes for the class. My teacher said I should ask my mum first.

STEP 2 (2.5 min) Practise

Which sentence shows that Orla is **most likely** to go to badminton practice?

Orla may go to badminton practice later. ☐

Orla could go to badminton practice later. ☐

Orla will go to badminton practice later. ☐

Orla ought to go to badminton practice later. ☐

Tip Some *adverbs* show degrees of certainty.

Underline the **adverb** that shows uncertainty in the sentence below.

Mum said perhaps we would visit our grandparents at the weekend but we definitely won't be able to stay long.

STEP 3 (1.5 min) Challenge

Write the **adverb** and **modal verb** in the sentence below that show certainty.

Theresa will definitely help you with your homework, although she may possibly struggle with the maths.

Adverb: _____   Modal verb: _____

Insert a different **adverb** to complete each sentence according to the degree of certainty indicated in the brackets.

We are _____ going camping this weekend. (uncertain)

The defender was _____ to blame for the bad tackle. (certain)

Date: _____

Day of week: _____

> **Tip** Most sentences are written in the **active voice**, where there is a subject, verb and optional object. In the **passive voice**, the subject undergoes the action of the verb.

> **Tip** The **passive voice** is formed from the past tense of the verb 'be' and the past participle of the main verb. Sometimes, the preposition 'by' is used. For example, The trip **was arranged by** the governors.

STEP 1 (1 min) Review

Which sentence is written in the **active voice**?

We were given two days to complete the science project. ☐

The baker skilfully kneaded the dough. ☐

Ben and Mohammad were taken to the first aid room. ☐

A new bread recipe was discussed at the team meeting. ☐

STEP 2 (2.5 min) Practise

Write these **active voice** sentences in the **passive voice**.

A news presenter interviewed the politician.

_____

The head teacher welcomed the visitor.

_____

An electrician repaired our broken dishwasher.

_____

The tree surgeon expertly felled the large oak.

_____

STEP 3 (1.5 min) Challenge

Tick **one** box in each row to show whether each sentence is written in the **active** or the **passive** voice.

Sentence	Active	Passive
The missing bracelet was found in the middle of the room.		
All the players were presented with an award.		
The referee was unsure whether the ball was off-side.		

Time spent: _____ min _____ sec. Total: _____ out of 8

STEP 1 (1 min) Review

- Rewrite the present tense verbs in the **simple past** on the line next to each.

  We **wait** _____ ages for the bus.

  Kaye **swims** _____ every morning on holiday.

- Label each box **S** for **subject** and **O** for **object**.

  The <u>judge</u> decided to award <u>the prize</u> to the comedy act.

  ↑   ↑

  [___]   [___]

STEP 2 (2.5 min) Practise

- Tick a box in each row to show the **tense** of each sentence.

Sentence	Present perfect	Past perfect	Present progressive	Past progressive
I've seen all the Harry Potter films.				
Mabel was eating breakfast with her mum.				
Tarek had forgotten his new neighbour's name.				
We are playing our new video game.				

STEP 3 (1.5 min) Challenge

- Rewrite the sentence below in the **passive voice**.

  The presenter introduced the celebrity.

  _____

- What is the **tense** of the underlined words in the sentence below?

  Nico <u>had thought</u> the test would be easier but how wrong he was.

  _____

- Rewrite the sentence below so that it is in the **active voice**.

  The prize was awarded to Class C by the head teacher.

  _____

21 Capital letters and full stops

Date: _____

Day of week: _____

Tip *A sentence starts with a **capital letter** and can end with a **full stop**, a question mark or an exclamation mark.*

STEP 1 (1 min) Review

Which sentence is correctly punctuated?

my teacher, Mr Agnew, is retiring in July. ☐

My Teacher, Mr Agnew, is retiring in July. ☐

My teacher, Mr Agnew, is retiring in July ☐

My teacher, Mr Agnew, is retiring in July. ☐

STEP 2 (2.5 min) Practise

Insert the **capital letters** and missing **full stops** in the passage below. The first one has been done for you.

W

ẉinnie and laura attend brighthill primary school they used to live in scotland but moved

here three years ago they both won a prize for music when they achieved high grades

in piano

STEP 3 (1.5 min) Challenge

Explain why the underlined words in the sentence below start with a **capital letter**.

I read *Harry Potter and the Philosopher's Stone* last September.

_____

_____

Rewrite the sentences below using the correct punctuation.

becky and i are going camping in the Summer we really hope the Sun shines for us

_____

_____

Time spent: _____ min _____ sec. Total: _____ out of 21

©HarperCollins*Publishers* 2021

Date: _____

Day of week: _____

Tip *Commas can be used to separate items in a list.*

STEP 1 (1 min) Review

Add **two commas** in the correct places in the sentence below.

Hal has dark brown eyes spiky hair with a fringe freckles and a dimple in one cheek.

Rewrite the sentence below using the correct punctuation.

Grace is, a brilliant netball player, athlete, musician, and artist.

_____

Tip *A **fronted adverbial** is always followed by a comma. When a **subordinate clause** comes at the start of a sentence, it is followed by a comma.*

STEP 2 (2.5 min) Practise

Add a **comma** to each sentence below.

If we were to get lost Dad could use his sat nav.

Should that not work we can phone for help.

However I think it's very unlikely we will lose our way.

After all Dad knows the area like the back of his hand!

Although he hasn't been here for a while he has an excellent memory.

Rewrite the sentence below so that it starts with the **subordinate clause**.

I really do hope we won't be long as the fuel tank is almost on empty.

_____

Tip *Commas can be used to avoid **ambiguity**, to make the intended meaning clear.*

STEP 3 (1.5 min) Challenge

Insert a **comma** in the sentence below to make it clear that the writer invited their parents and Euan and Amber for lunch.

I invited my parents Euan and Amber for lunch at the weekend.

Insert **commas** in the sentence below to make it clear that the writer invited their parents who are called Euan and Amber for lunch.

I invited my parents Euan and Amber for lunch at the weekend.

Date: _____

Day of week: _____

Tip *The closing **inverted commas** come **after** the final punctuation of the direct speech.*

STEP 1 (1 min) Review

Tick **two** boxes to show where the missing **inverted commas** should go.

Why is a dog man's best friend? Julian asked his granddad.

☐   ☐   ☐   ☐

STEP 2 (2.5 min) Practise

Insert the missing punctuation in the direct speech below.

I really liked the concert last night said Mia. The guitarists were amazing

Yes, they were exclaimed Alex. Though I was particularly impressed by the drummer

Would you be interested in taking up guitar lessons with me asked Mia

When we get home replied Alex we'll ask Mum

STEP 3 (1.5 min) Challenge

Which **two** pieces of advice would you give to correct the punctuation of the sentence below?

"We need to hurry or we shall miss the bus", Said Bertha.

The second pair of inverted commas should come after the comma.   ☐

There should be an exclamation mark after the word 'bus'.   ☐

The word 'Said' should start with a lower case 's'.   ☐

The second pair of inverted commas should come after 'Bertha'.   ☐

Time spent: _____ min _____ sec. Total: _____ out of 27   ©HarperCollins*Publishers* 2021

Tip To indicate possession in a singular noun, the **apostrophe** is placed after the last letter of the noun and before the letter **'s'**. For example, the **dog's** tail.

STEP 1 (1 min) Review

Insert an **apostrophe** to show possession for each underlined noun.

The <u>hotels</u> guests were delighted with its new facilities.

My <u>brothers</u> friends are even noisier than he is.

We wouldn't dare sit on our <u>teachers</u> chair!

<u>Dads</u> expensive oil paints are kept locked in a drawer.

STEP 2 (2.5 min) Practise

Tip To indicate possession in a plural noun, the **apostrophe** is placed **after** the letter **'s'**. For example, the **dogs'** tails. Watch out for irregular plurals such as 'men'!

Tick **one** box in each row to show whether the underlined noun is **singular** or **plural**.

Sentence	Singular	Plural
The servants presented the <u>prince's</u> crown on a velvet cushion.		
The <u>horses'</u> hooves were checked before the gymkhana.		
The <u>men's</u> changing room has been repainted.		

Circle the word in the sentence that contains an **apostrophe** for possession.

We'd been looking for Mum's keys for ages but we couldn't find them anywhere.

STEP 3 (1.5 min) Challenge

Insert an **apostrophe** in the correct place in each sentence below.

James feet have grown two whole sizes!

The guests desserts were brought out with their coffee.

Tip To show possession in proper names ending in **'s'**, the **apostrophe** can come **after** the **final 's'** or **after** the **final 's'** followed by **another 's'**. For example, **Chris'** shoes / **Chris's** shoes.

Explain how the position of the **apostrophe** changes the meaning from the first sentence to the second sentence.

I like your sister's new gloves.   I like your sisters' new gloves.

_____

Tip *An **apostrophe** in a contraction is placed where the missed out letter or letters would have been. For example, **I'm** pleased to see you.*

STEP 1 (1 min) **Review**

Write the full form of each contraction.

could've _____   she's _____

hadn't _____   I've _____

we'd _____   can't _____

they're _____   Chloe's _____

STEP 2 (2.5 min) **Practise**

Write the contracted forms of the underlined words in the sentences below.

<u>Do not</u> expect me to help you to tidy up that mess!   _____

<u>Ellie has</u> been feeling sick for a couple of days.   _____

I said <u>they would</u> complete the marathon in record time.   _____

I <u>shall not</u> be going to the play as I'm busy that night.   _____

STEP 3 (1.5 min) **Challenge**

Tick a box on each row to show whether the **apostrophe** has been used to show possession or a contraction.

Sentence	Possession	Contraction
Dylan turned out to be one of our family's distant cousins.		
We decided there'd be no point in going out as it was raining.		
That girl's been annoying me all day.		
Fabian's school bag mysteriously reappeared on his chair.		

Time spent: _____ min _____ sec. Total: _____ out of 16   ©HarperCollins*Publishers* 2021

Date: _____

Day of week: _____

Tip *Parenthesis is additional information added to a sentence. It is shown by parentheses, the punctuation that comes before and after the word, phrase or clause in parenthesis.*

STEP 1 (1 min) **Review**

Which sentence is punctuated correctly?

Our homework a project – on rivers – has to be submitted tomorrow. ☐

Our homework a project on rivers – has to be submitted – tomorrow. ☐

Our homework – a project on rivers – has to be submitted tomorrow. ☐

Our homework a project – on rivers has to be submitted – tomorrow. ☐

STEP 2 (2.5 min) **Practise**

Underline the words that are in **parenthesis** in the sentence below.

My best friend's dad, originally from Thailand, makes an amazing coconut curry.

What is the name of the parentheses on either side of the words either monkfish or cod in the sentence below?

He makes it with fish – either monkfish or cod – and a range of unusual spices.

_____

What is the name of the parentheses on either side of the words his granddad lives there in the sentence below?

Han is going to Thailand for Easter (his granddad lives there) and I'm delighted to say he's invited me to join him.

_____

STEP 3 (1.5 min) **Challenge**

Insert a pair of brackets in the correct places in the sentence below.

Pilar speaks Spanish her parents are from Madrid but her sister barely understands a word.

Insert a suitable parenthetic phrase in the sentence below.

Our neighbour _____ is preparing for his retirement.

Date: _____

Day of week: _____

Tip *A semi-colon can be used to link two closely related independent clauses.*

STEP 1 (1 min) Review

Which sentence uses the **semi-colon** correctly?

The runners were relaxing; in the spa it had been a competitive race. ☐

The runners were relaxing in the spa; it had been a competitive race. ☐

The runners; were relaxing in the spa it had been a competitive race. ☐

The runners were relaxing in the spa it had been; a competitive race. ☐

STEP 2 (2.5 min) Practise

Insert a **semi-colon** in each sentence below.

Phillip takes two sugars in his tea however, I don't take any.

The boat sailed smoothly away from the island there was a light breeze and a calm sea.

We've been going on camping holidays for years we wouldn't do anything else.

It might be time to buy a new car our current one keeps breaking down.

STEP 3 (1.5 min) Challenge

Which sentence does **not** use the **semi-colon** correctly?

Matthew and Rory are both vegetarian; Kate and Lisa are vegan. ☐

Painting is Mum's favourite pastime; her most recent creation is on the wall. ☐

The team has achieved amazing success; since signing Mike he truly is a great defender. ☐

Javid has had his hair cut; he reckons the new barber is really good. ☐

Time spent: _____ min _____ sec. Total: _____ out of 6

Tip *A **colon** can introduce an explanation, a list or a quote.*

STEP 1 (1 min) Review

Insert a **colon** in the correct place in each sentence below.

On holiday, we did all sorts of activities we went swimming, snorkelling and water-skiing, as well as rock climbing and hiking.

Juliet O Romeo, Romeo, wherefore art thou Romeo?

From the top of the mountain we saw the most amazing view a shimmering lake, a river and a church spire nestled in some trees.

I told Jake how to make flapjacks mix the oats, honey and melted butter together, place in a baking tray and bake for 30 minutes.

STEP 2 (2.5 min) Practise

Inserting a **colon** and **bullet points**, use the words in the box to write the start of a recipe for biscuits.

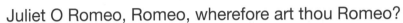

You will need the following 300g flour 150g butter 100g sugar 1 egg

_____

_____   _____

_____   _____

STEP 3 (1.5 min) Challenge

Which sentence uses a **colon** correctly?

There were many reasons for Naomi's bad mood: she was tired and hungry, and she'd been told off for talking in class. ☐

There were many reasons: for Naomi's bad mood she was tired and hungry, and she'd been told off for talking in class. ☐

There were many reasons for Naomi's bad mood she was tired and hungry: and she'd been told off for talking in class. ☐

There were many reasons for Naomi's bad mood she was tired and hungry, and she'd been told off: for talking in class. ☐

> **Tip** A *single dash* can be used at the start of a clause that adds additional information to the preceding clause. It can also be used for dramatic effect or to signal an interruption.

STEP 1 (1 min) Review

Which sentence below uses a **dash** correctly?

As I walked round the corner, I gasped in shock – it was him again! ☐

As I walked round the corner, I gasped – in shock it was him again! ☐

As I walked round – the corner, I gasped in shock it was him again! ☐

As I walked round the corner, I gasped in shock it was him – again! ☐

> **Tip** A **hyphen** can be used to join **two or more** words together as a compound word or to join a prefix to a word where the prefix ends in a vowel and the initial letter of the word starts with a vowel.

STEP 2 (2.5 min) Practise

Write **D** or **H** in each box to indicate whether each arrow is pointing to a **dash** or a **hyphen**.

It will soon be my birthday – I really hope I get the high-tech version of the video game!

Insert **two hyphens** in the sentence below to form compound words.

Bavini prefers sugar free drinks whereas her sister eats full fat yoghurt.

STEP 3 (1.5 min) Challenge

Tick **one** box to show where a **hyphen** should be inserted in the sentence below.

Our school caretaker did a first class job of clearing up the fallen leaves.

Match each word or letter on the left with the correct word in the middle column of the table. Write each **hyphenated** word in the right-hand column of the table.

Word / letter	Word	Hyphenated word
co	ray	
empty	tech	
e	operate	
high	handed	
X	mail	

Time spent: _____ min _____ sec. Total: _____ out of 11

©HarperCollins*Publishers* 2021

STEP 1 (1 min) Review

- Rewrite the sentences below using the correct punctuation.

  nicky is going Skiing this Winter she's nervous as she's never left the united kingdom before

  _____

  _____

- Insert a **comma** in the sentence below to show that Fiona likes doing **three** things.

  Fiona likes cooking her pets and reading.

- Insert a **comma** in the sentence below to show that the speaker is asking Andrea to help tidy up.

  We need help to tidy up Andrea.

STEP 2 (2.5 min) Practise

- Insert a **semi-colon** in the sentence below.

  Mum needs your help in the garden I've already swept up the leaves.

- Insert a pair of **dashes** in the sentence below.

  James a highly regarded World War II pilot has sadly died.

- Insert an **apostrophe** in each sentence to show possession.

  The teachers felt that the childrens behaviour could have been better.

  We went through the door that said 'Womens Showers'.

STEP 3 (1.5 min) Challenge

- Insert the missing punctuation in the direct speech sentence below.

  Are you going to join us for the picnic Gwyn asked Ted.

- Insert **three commas** and a **semi-colon** in the correct places in the passage below.

  At the museum we saw various Egyptian artefacts learnt to write hieroglyphics watched a short video about Cleopatra and made models of pyramids it truly was the most amazing day!

Date: _____

Day of week: _____

Tip *Standard English means using correct grammar. It can be formal or informal.*

STEP 1 (1 min) **Review**

Which sentence is **not** written in **Standard English**?

I'm going to be a bridesmaid at my aunt's wedding. ☐

I haven't done nothing like that before. ☐

It'll be so cool! ☐

It'll be fun to see so many family members. ☐

STEP 2 (2.5 min) **Practise**

Underline the correct word in each box to complete the sentences in **Standard English**.

The doctor gave Dan | them / those | tablets for his headaches.

Sean | done / did | his homework in record time.

I | seen / saw | a famous actor walking down the road.

My sister doesn't have | no / any | money to buy sweets.

STEP 3 (1.5 min) **Challenge**

Rewrite the passage below so that it is in **Standard English**.

"I've not done nothing wrong," said Rob.

But the teacher seen him scribble on the table and she were getting more crosser.

"If you ain't done it, Rob, I don't have no clue who it could have been!"

_____

_____

_____

Time spent: _____ min _____ sec. Total: _____ out of 11

Tip *Formal writing* does not include slang or colloquial words.

STEP 1 (1 min) Review

Which sentence is the most **formal**?

I wish you'd get those documents back quickly. ☐

I expect you to return the documents punctually. ☐

Can't you get those documents back to me ASAP? ☐

Hurry up and get those documents back to me! ☐

STEP 2 (2.5 min) Practise

Underline the most **formal** sentence in the passage below.

I really hope you enjoy our show this evening. The children have worked really hard and can't wait to show off their amazing talent. But first, a safety announcement. Should you hear the fire alarm, please proceed to the rear of the building.

 Tip *The **subjunctive** is used to express a wish, a demand or a hypothetical situation. For example, If I **were** you, I'd accept the job.*

STEP 3 (1.5 min) Challenge

Which word completes the sentence so that it is in the **subjunctive**?

I dreamt I'd won a million pounds! If only it _____ true.

was ☐   are ☐

is ☐   were ☐

Insert a suitable word to complete each sentence so that it is in the **subjunctive**.

Should you ____ cold, please switch on the heating.

The judge demanded that the prisoner _____ brought before her.

Date: _____

Day of week: _____

> **Tip** A **synonym** is a word with the same or almost the same meaning as another word.
>
> An **antonym** is a word that has an opposite meaning to another word.

STEP 1 (1 min) Review

Draw a line to join each word to its **synonym**.

dawn	escape
register	deliberate
applaud	sunrise
purposeful	clap
flee	record

STEP 2 (2.5 min) Practise

Underline **two** words in the passage that are **synonyms** of each other.

We knew it would be cloudy as the forecast had said so. However, despite the overcast skies, the temperature was pleasant and there was a warm breeze.

Underline **two** words in the passage that are **antonyms** of each other.

Our new kitchen is very contemporary with its high-tech oven and plasma TV; our previous one now seems so antiquated.

STEP 3 (1.5 min) Challenge

Which word below is an **antonym** of 'accept'?

Dev wrote to <u>accept</u> the invitation.

deny ☐

refuse ☐

dispute ☐

receive ☐

Which noun is a **synonym** of the noun 'assembly'?

greeting ☐   gathering ☐   sing-a-long ☐   worship ☐

Date: _____

Day of week: _____

Tip   *A prefix does not change the spelling of the word it is added to.*

STEP 1 (1 min) Review

What does the **prefix** '**sub-**' mean in the following words?

submarine	**subway**	**subheading**

above ☐

below ☐

around ☐

in between ☐

STEP 2 (2.5 min) Practise

Draw a line to match each word with the correct **prefix** to create a word with the opposite meaning.

in-   guided

de-   practical

mis-   respect

im-   regular

un-   complete

dis-   forgiving

ir-   compose

STEP 3 (1.5 min) Challenge

Add a **prefix** to each of the words in **bold**.

I bought the Olympic medallist's _____**biography** last week. It's an

_____**national** bestseller. I'm _____**patient** to start reading it and I suspect

I'll be rather _____**social** for a while!

35 Suffixes (1)

Date: _____

Day of week: _____

Tip The **suffixes '-ant', '-ance'** and **'-ancy'** are used if there is a related word with an **'-ation'** ending. For example, application → applicant.

STEP 1 (1 min) Review

Add the suffixes '**-ant**' and '**-ance**' to the following words.

Word	'-ant'	'-ance'
observe		
hesitate		
tolerate		

STEP 2 (2.5 min) Practise

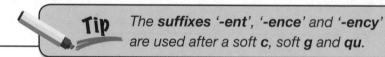

Tip The **suffixes '-ent', '-ence'** and **'-ency'** are used after a soft **c**, soft **g** and **qu**.

Underline the correct spelling in each word pair in the sentences below.

There has been an alarming **frequency / frequancy** of accidents outside our local supermarket.

Despite the fact that his hands were covered in red paint, Blake protested his **innocance / innocence**.

"If you can't make it, at least have the **decency / decancy** to let me know!" complained Markus.

STEP 3 (1.5 min) Challenge

Some words do not follow the spelling guidance. Add the suffixes '**-ant**', '**-ance**' or '**-ent**', '**-ence**' to the following words.

Word	'-ant'	'-ance'	'-ent'	'-ence'
assist				
obey				
differ				
insist				
comply				
coincide				

Time spent: _____ min _____ sec. Total: _____ out of 21

Date: _____

Day of week: _____

Tip *The 'ubel' and 'ubly' sounds can be spelt '-able' and '-ably' or '-ible' and '-ibly'. These suffixes can be added to verbs and nouns to turn them into adjectives and adverbs. The '-able' and '-ably' endings are often used if a complete root word can be heard before them.*

STEP 1 (1 min) Review

Underline the word that is spelt correctly in each pair.

dependable / dependible   incredible / incredable   comfortable / comfortible

reasonable / reasonible   enjoyable / enjoyible   horrable / horrible

STEP 2 (2.5 min) Practise

 Tip *Use '-able' and '-ably' if there is a related word with an '-ation' ending.*

Turn these verbs and nouns into adjectives and adverbs.

Verb	Noun	Adjective	Adverb
consider	consideration		
tolerate	toleration		
adore	adoration		
demonstrate	demonstration		

 Tip *If adding '-able' to a verb or noun ending in ce or ge, the letter e that comes after these endings must be kept in the word to keep the sound 'soft'.*

STEP 3 (1.5 min) Challenge

Choose either '-able' or '-ible' to turn these verbs into adjectives.

force   _____

change   _____

notice   _____

rely   _____

recognise   _____

vision   _____

Time spent: _____ min _____ sec. Total: _____ out of 19

Date: _____

Day of week: _____

Tip *To help you learn to spell these words, try pronouncing the **silent letter** in your head.*

STEP 1 (1 min) **Review**

Circle the **silent letter** in each word below.

island	honourable	column	doubtful	receipt
hour	knuckles	psychologist	Wednesday	castle

STEP 2 (2.5 min) **Practise**

Rewrite each word on the line provided, inserting the missing **silent letter**.

nock	goverment	parlament	caf	eir
_____	_____	_____	_____	_____

com	lisen	busle	samon	reconise
_____	_____	_____	_____	_____

STEP 3 (1.5 min) **Challenge**

Find the **six** words in the passage that have been spelt as they sound. Write their correct spellings on the lines below.

Last year, we travelled to a remote iland off the coast of Ireland. The senery was stunning and the village fok were very welcoming. We rented a yat (£50 for haf a day) and sailed to the northern point where we new there was a little cove.

1. _____   2. _____

3. _____   4. _____

5. _____   6. _____

Tip The digraph '**ei**' can make an '**ee**', '**ay**', '**ih**' (as in sover**ei**gn) or '**i**' sound (as in h**ei**ght). Usually '**ei**' is used after the letter '**c**' if the sound made is '**ee**'. The digraph '**ie**' usually makes an '**ee**' sound (as in br**ie**f). Watch out for unusual exceptions such as 'sc**ie**nce'.

STEP 1 (1 min) Review

Insert the missing vowel digraph in each word below.

rec_ _ ve   c_ _ ling   conc_ _ ve   dec_ _ t   perc_ _ ve

rec_ _ pt   h_ _ ght   b _ _ ge   _ _ ght

STEP 2 (2.5 min) Practise

Find the **five** incorrectly spelt words in the box and write them correctly below.

piece	sceince	foreign	sieve	brief	shreik	wierd
	chief	grief	glaceir	concieted		

_____   _____   _____

_____   _____

STEP 3 (1.5 min) Challenge

Solve the clues to find words with the '**ie**' and '**ei**' digraphs.

Important for a healthy diet.

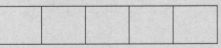

A female family relative.

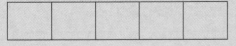

To grab hold of.

The blockade of a city and the cutting off of its supplies.

Tip A **homophone** is a word that sounds the same as another word but has a different spelling and meaning.

A **near-homophone** sounds **almost** the same as another word.

STEP 1 (1 min) Review

Write the **homophone** for each word below.

aisle _____   seen _____   threw _____

Write the **near-homophone** for each word below.

quite _____   effect _____   advice _____

STEP 2 (2.5 min) Practise

Choose a **homophone** or **near-homophone** from the box below to complete the passage.

wondered / wandered	proceed / precede	our / are	beech / beach
poring / pouring	fare / fair	whether / weather	

We _____ if we should _____ with _____

plan to go to the _____ as it was _____ down. However, it

wasn't long before the _____ _____ returned.

STEP 3 (1.5 min) Challenge

Write a sentence for each of the following **homophones**.

threw

_____

through

_____

compliment

_____

complement

_____

Time spent: _____ min _____ sec. Total: _____ out of 17   ©HarperCollins*Publishers* 2021

STEP 1 (1 min) Review

- Underline the correct spelling in each word pair in the sentences below.

  Shona mixed the **substence / substance** in the beaker.

  We held a one-minute silence in **remembrance / rememberence** of those who died.

- Add a prefix to each word below to form its **antonym**.

  ___conceivable   ___regard

  ___material   ___legible

- Underline the most **formal** sentence in the passage below.

  It is with regret that I have to inform you that Mr Williams will retire effective next month. We'll all miss him terribly. He's always been really popular with pupils and staff alike and has a mischievous sense of humour, as you all know.

STEP 2 (2.5 min) Practise

- Underline the **two** words that are **synonyms**.

  dismal   furious   bleak   upset   annoying

- Underline the **two** words that are **antonyms**.

  grateful   brave   inquisitive   unconcerned   reserved

- Add **able** or **ible** to each word below.

  love _____   flex _____

  resist _____   desire _____

STEP 3 (1.5 min) Challenge

- Write the **homophone** for each word below.

  alter _____   whale _____   aloud _____

- Write the **near-homophone** for each word below.

  device _____   desert _____   stationery _____

- Underline the verb that is in the **subjunctive mood** in the sentence below.

  I demand Mr Robinson be present at the council committee meeting this evening.

ANSWERS

Test 1

Step 1:

The <u>children</u> walked to <u>school</u> because it was warm and sunny.

There are plenty of <u>paints</u> in the <u>cupboard</u> if you look hard.

When they saw the <u>glimmering</u> light, they were <u>hopeful</u> someone was in the cottage.

Arriving at our <u>final</u> destination, we were <u>thrilled</u> to find there was a funfair.

Step 2:

<u>fear</u>; <u>determination</u>; <u>quest</u>

Step 3:

Last May, Mr Thomas visited Madagascar in the Indian Ocean. ✓

Test 2

Step 1:

Accept any suitable adjective, e.g. **beautiful** butterflies, **noisy** parrots, **cheeky** monkeys, **glittering** stars.

Step 2:

<u>the interesting talk delivered by the explorer</u>.

<u>Some naughty children from Class B</u>

<u>an iced sponge cake topped with eleven candles</u>.

<u>the bag containing a hoard of stolen jewellery</u>.

Step 3:

Any suitable sentence containing an expanded noun phrase.

Test 3

Step 1:

We <u>packed</u> our bags and <u>loaded</u> the car.

Mum <u>used</u> kindling to <u>light</u> the campfire.

Eva <u>has</u> a bad cold so she <u>is going</u> to bed early.

"I <u>have</u> two cats and a dog," Xavier <u>told</u> me.

Step 2:

Viktor worked hard on his times tables revision. ✓

The teachers lead the children into the playground. ✓

Step 3:

adverb; adjective; noun

Test 4

Step 1:

We packed our waterproofs <u>and</u> boots <u>because</u> rain was predicted over the weekend.

<u>Although</u> we don't have high-tech computers <u>or</u> up-to-date gym equipment, our school is amazing.

Step 2:

Sentence	Main clause	Subordinate clause
We watched the new Harry Potter film <u>after we celebrated Dad's birthday</u>.		✓
As neither of us were wearing a watch, <u>Vim and I missed the last bus</u>.	✓	
Although my alarm clock hadn't yet gone off, <u>I got up</u>.	✓	
The children took shelter under a large oak tree <u>so that they wouldn't get wet</u>.		✓

Step 3:

Millie's gran cooks **while** she listens to the radio. Also accept: '**as**'.

When she realised she had forgotten her homework**,** Sarah ran back to the house.

Test 5

Step 1:

Sentence	Main clause	Relative clause
<u>We played the game</u> which you bought us for Christmas.	✓	
Our Irish cousins, <u>with whom we are going on holiday,</u> are great fun.		✓
<u>There's the man</u> whose house burnt down last month.	✓	
The musical <u>I wanted to see</u> has sold out.		✓

Step 2:

The caretaker, **whose** shed is in the playground, was annoyed to find it had been vandalised.

Mrs Kamal, **who** is my teacher, is very kind and patient.

The hospital **where** Dad was born is now derelict.

"To **whom** does this book belong?" asked our teacher.

Step 3:

Accept any suitable relative clause, e.g.

Maria, **who sits next to me**, speaks Spanish.

The book **that you gave me** was brilliant.

Our new car keeps breaking down, **which is such a disappointment**.

Test 6

Step 1:

<u>We</u>; <u>I</u>; <u>you</u>; <u>it</u>

Step 2:

he; they; we; it

Step 3:

him; me; it; her; me; I

Test 7

Step 1:

<u>yours</u>; <u>theirs</u>; <u>mine</u>; <u>yours</u>

Step 2:

Pronouns		Possessive pronouns
I	them	yours
you	She	Ours
it	him	theirs
We	he	his

Step 3:

He; him; she; he; them

Test 8

Step 1:

<u>across</u>; <u>on</u>; <u>in</u>; <u>under</u>

Step 2:

Mum drove **around / round** the roundabout until she found the right exit.

The balloon sailed **in / into / through** the air above us.

Ciara tiptoed **towards** the sleeping baby.

Dad wrote his signature **at / on** the bottom of the form.

Naomi met Euan **at** six o'clock.

Step 3:

The spider crawled <u>along</u> the window sill, <u>up</u> the curtain and back <u>to</u> its web <u>in</u> the corner.

Before we leave home, we usually activate the alarm. ✓

Test 9

Step 1:

We watched <u>a</u> policeman chase <u>two</u> criminals.

We ate <u>some</u> fruit after we had finished <u>the</u> pizza.

I think <u>this</u> book is better than <u>that</u> one.

<u>These</u> chocolate biscuits are better than <u>those</u> coconut creams.

Step 2:

[My] dad kindly said I could borrow [his] computer as mine is broken.

Wendy took a photo of [her] dog and sent it to [my] big brother.

[Your] new coat suits you and I like [your] matching scarf.

"Do you want sauce on [your] chips?" Ben asked [his] younger brother.

Step 3:

Accept any suitable determiners, e.g.

I have **three** felt pens and **six** colouring pencils.

At the zoo, we saw **an** elephant and **an** orangutan.

Gabby slipped on **some** wet moss and hurt **her** knee.

There are **many** reasons why I don't like sprouts and **the** smell is just one!

Test 10: Progress Test 1

Step 1:

A suitable adverb, e.g. The dogs ran **quickly** towards the river.

The **R**iver **T**hames runs through **L**ondon and is 215 miles long**.**

A noun phrase / an expanded noun phrase.

Step 2:

The divers swam <u>through</u> an underwater cave and emerged <u>on</u> the other side.

determiners ✓

Relative clause

Possessive pronoun

Step 3:

Conjunctions / subordinating conjunctions

Floyd approached the gaping mouth of the cave; he stopped abruptly and considered **his** options.

verb; noun

Test 11

Step 1:

<u>Sheena</u>; <u>The park keeper</u>; <u>They</u>; <u>Huge waves</u>

Step 2:

(the pepper); (the seeds); (the car); (a long queue)

Step 3:

"Will the boys come to the staffroom at lunchtime, please?"

| S | | O |

announced the teacher.

Ethan bought a blue hat with his pocket money and

| S | | O |

he gave it to his brother.

| S | O |

Test 12

Step 1:

What was the result of your maths test ✓

Any suitable statement, correctly punctuated.

Step 2:

Has Ben finished his homework on time this week?

Any suitable question, correctly punctuated, e.g How many pets do you have?

Step 3:

Any suitable question, correctly punctuated.

Test 13

Step 1:

Please bring your PE kit to school tomorrow. ✓

Any suitable command, correctly punctuated, e.g. Please help me lift this.

Step 2:

<u>Switch</u> on your tablet and <u>press</u> the link to the wildlife website.

What a lot of noise you're making! ✓

Any suitable exclamation sentence, correctly punctuated, e.g. What a wonderful present this is!

Step 3:

When will you have completed the jigsaw ✓

Test 14

Step 1:

The performers take position on stage and wait for the music to start. ✓

Accept any suitable verb in the simple past tense, e.g. Zac painted a picture and **gave** it to his mum.

Step 2:

lay; ate; recharges; feel

Step 3:

greet; are; invite; accept; wait; pitch; freshen

Test 15

Step 1:

have been ✓

Accept any suitable verb in the present perfect tense, e.g. Enda **has finished** his homework at long last!

Step 2:

had tried; had been; had ignored; had seen

Step 3:

Our grandparents have a caravan now. ✓

Test 16

Step 1:

Mum is hanging up the picture. ✓

Any suitable verb in the present progressive tense, e.g. The teachers **are showing** the visitors around the school.

Step 2:

We <u>are helping</u> Dad clear the garden shed. He asked us ages ago but we have always made excuses! We <u>are throwing</u> all the junk into a skip while Dad <u>is tidying</u> his tools. He <u>is being</u> particularly fussy about keeping the ones that had belonged to his grandfather.

Step 3:

Sentence	Simple present	Simple past	Present progressive
The geese are migrating from Iceland towards the east coast of Scotland.			✓
We watch them through our binoculars.	✓		
Last year, they arrived in early September.		✓	

Test 17

Step 1:

Sentence	Present progressive	Past progressive
The royal family is gathering on the balcony to greet the crowd.	✓	

			✓
Jaime was being unkind to his sister at breakfast.			✓
I'm having some friends round for pizza tonight.		✓	

Step 2:
was going; was standing; was raining; was meeting
Accept any suitable sentence in the past progressive tense.

Step 3:
We were waiting ages for the train. ✓
Meg **was going** to the gym to search for her missing PE kit.
Accept any suitable sentence using the verb form **'was learning'** or **'were learning'**.

Test 18

Step 1:
can ; must ; could ; should

Step 2:
Orla will go to badminton practice later. ✓
Mum said perhaps we would visit our grandparents at the weekend but we definitely won't be able to stay long.

Step 3:
Adverb: **definitely**   Modal verb: **will**
Accept any suitable adverbs. For example:
We are **possibly** going camping this weekend. (uncertain)
The defender was **undoubtedly** to blame for the bad tackle. (certain)

Test 19

Step 1:
The baker skilfully kneaded the dough. ✓

Step 2:
The politician was interviewed by a news presenter.
The visitor was welcomed by the head teacher.
Our broken dishwasher was repaired by an electrician.
The large oak was expertly felled by the tree surgeon.

Step 3:

Sentence	Active	Passive
The missing bracelet was found in the middle of the room.		✓
All the players were presented with an award.		✓
The referee was unsure whether the ball was off-side.	✓	

Test 20: Progress Test 2

Step 1:
waited; swam

The judge decided to award the prize to the comedy act.

    ┌── S ──┐   ┌── O ──┐

Step 2:

Sentence	Present perfect	Past perfect	Present progressive	Past progressive
I've seen all the Harry Potter films.	✓			
Mabel was eating breakfast with her mum.				✓

		✓	
Tarek had forgotten his new neighbour's name.		✓	
We are playing our new video game.			✓

Step 3:
The celebrity was introduced by the presenter.
Past perfect
The head teacher awarded the prize to Class C.

Test 21

Step 1:
My teacher, Mr Agnew, is retiring in July. ✓

Step 2:
        W   L   B   P   S   T
winnie and laura attend brighthill primary school. they used to live
        S   T
in scotland but moved here three years ago. they both won a prize for music when they achieved high grades in piano.

Step 3:
'I' is always written with a capital letter.
Harry Potter and the Philosopher's Stone is a book title / proper noun.
September is a month of the year / proper noun.
Becky and **I** are going camping in the **s**ummer. **W**e really hope the **s**un shines for us.

Test 22

Step 1:
Hal has dark brown eyes, spiky hair with a fringe, freckles and a dimple in one cheek.
Grace is a brilliant netball player, athlete, musician and artist.

Step 2:
If we were to get lost, Dad could use his sat nav.
Should that not work, we can phone for help.
However, I think it's very unlikely we will lose our way.
After all, Dad knows the area like the back of his hand!
Although he hasn't been here for a while, he has an excellent memory.
As the fuel tank is almost on empty, I really do hope we won't be long.

Step 3:
I invited my parents, Euan and Amber for lunch at the weekend.
I invited my parents, Euan and Amber, for lunch at the weekend.

Test 23

Step 1:
Why is a dog man's best friend? Julian asked his granddad.

Step 2:
"I really liked the concert last night," said Mia. "The guitarists were amazing."
"Yes, they were!" exclaimed Alex. "Though I was particularly impressed by the drummer." (Also accept: "Yes, they were,")
"Would you be interested in taking up guitar lessons with me?" asked Mia.
"When we get home," replied Alex, "we'll ask Mum."

Step 3:
The second pair of inverted commas should come after the comma. ✓
The word 'Said' should start with a lower case 's'. ✓

Test 24

Step 1:
The hotel's guests were delighted with its new facilities.
My brother's friends are even noisier than he is.

We wouldn't dare sit on our <u>teacher's</u> chair!

<u>Dad's</u> expensive oil paints are kept locked in a drawer.

Step 2:

Sentence	Singular	Plural
The servants presented the <u>prince's</u> crown on a velvet cushion.	✓	
The <u>horses'</u> hooves were checked before the gymkhana.		✓
The <u>men's</u> changing room has been repainted.		✓

We'd been looking for <u>Mum's</u> keys for ages but we couldn't find them anywhere.

Step 3:
James' feet have grown two whole sizes! Also accept: James's.

The guests' desserts were brought out with their coffee.

The writer is referring to more than one sister in the second sentence.

Test 25

Step 1:

could have	she is / has
had not	I have
we had / would	can not / cannot
they are	Chloe is / has

Step 2:
Don't; Ellie's; they'd; shan't

Step 3:

Sentence	Possession	Contraction
Dylan turned out to be one of our family's distant cousins.	✓	
We decided there'd be no point in going out as it was raining.		✓
That girl's been annoying me all day.		✓
Fabian's school bag mysteriously reappeared on his chair.	✓	

Test 26

Step 1:
Our homework – a project on rivers – has to be submitted tomorrow. ✓

Step 2:
My best friend's dad, <u>originally from Thailand</u>, makes an amazing coconut curry.

Dashes

Brackets

Step 3:
Pilar speaks Spanish (her parents are from Madrid) but her sister barely understands a word.

Accept any suitable parenthetic phrase, e.g.

Our neighbour, **who has just turned sixty,** is preparing for his retirement.

Test 27

Step 1:
The runners were relaxing in the spa; it had been a competitive race. ✓

Step 2:
Phillip takes two sugars in his tea; however, I don't take any.

The boat sailed smoothly away from the island; there was a light breeze and a calm sea.

We've been going on camping holidays for years; we wouldn't do anything else.

It might be time to buy a new car; our current one keeps breaking down.

Step 3:
The team has achieved amazing success; since signing Mike he truly is a great defender. ✓

Test 28

Step 1:
On holiday, we did all sorts of activities: we went swimming, snorkelling and water-skiing, as well as rock climbing and hiking.

Juliet: O Romeo, Romeo, wherefore art thou Romeo?

From the top of the mountain we saw the most amazing view: a shimmering lake, a river and a church spire nestled in some trees.

I told Jake how to make flapjacks: mix the oats, honey and melted butter together, place in a baking tray and bake for 30 minutes.

Step 2:
You will need the following:
- 300g flour
- 150g butter
- 100g sugar
- 1 egg

Step 3:
There were many reasons for Naomi's bad mood: she was tired and hungry, and she'd been told off for talking in class. ✓

Test 29

Step 1:
As I walked round the corner, I gasped in shock – it was him again! ✓

Step 2:
It will soon be my birthday – I really hope I get the high-tech

version of the video game! Bavini prefers **sugar-free** drinks whereas her sister eats **full-fat** yoghurt.

Step 3:
Our school caretaker did a first class job of clearing up the fallen leaves.

co-operate; empty-handed; e-mail; high-tech; X-ray

Test 30: Progress Test 3

Step 1:
Nicky is going **s**kiing this **w**inter. **S**he's nervous as she's never left the **U**nited **K**ingdom before.

Fiona likes cooking, her pets and reading.

We need help to tidy up, Andrea.

Step 2:
Mum needs your help in the garden; I've already swept up the leaves.

James – a highly regarded World War II pilot – has sadly died.

The teachers felt that the children's behaviour could have been better.

We went through the door that said 'Women's Showers'.

Step 3:
"Are you going to join us for the picnic?" Gwyn asked Ted. / "Are you going to join us for the picnic, Gwyn?" asked Ted.

At the museum, we saw various Egyptian artefacts, learnt to write hieroglyphics, watched a short video about Cleopatra and made models of pyramids; it truly was the most amazing day!

Test 31

Step 1:
I haven't done nothing like that before. ✓

Step 2:
The doctor gave Dan them / <u>those</u> tablets for his headaches.

Sean done / <u>did</u> his homework in record time.

I seen / <u>saw</u> a famous actor walking down the road.

My sister doesn't have no / <u>any</u> money to buy sweets.

Step 3:
"I've not done **anything** wrong," said Rob.

But the teacher **had** seen him scribble on the table and she **was** getting more **cross** / getting **crosser**.

"If you **haven't** done it, Rob, I don't have **a** clue who it could have been!"

Test 32

Step 1:

I expect you to return the documents punctually. ✓

Step 2:

I really hope you enjoy our show this evening. The children have worked really hard and can't wait to show off their amazing talent. But first, a safety announcement. <u>Should you hear the fire alarm, please proceed to the rear of the building.</u>

Step 3:

were ✓

Should you **be** cold, please switch on the heating.

The judge demanded that the prisoner **be** brought before her.

Test 33

Step 1:

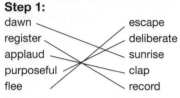

dawn — sunrise
register — record
applaud — clap
purposeful — deliberate
flee — escape

Step 2:

We knew it would be <u>cloudy</u> as the forecast had said so. However, despite the <u>overcast</u> skies, the temperature was pleasant and there was a warm breeze.

Our new kitchen is very <u>contemporary</u> with its high-tech oven and plasma TV; our old one now seems so <u>antiquated</u>.

Step 3:

refuse ✓

gathering ✓

Test 34

Step 1:

below ✓

Step 2:

incomplete; **de**compose; **mis**guided; **im**practical; **un**forgiving; **dis**respect; **ir**regular

Step 3:

I bought the Olympic medallist's **autobiography** last week. It's an **international** bestseller. I'm **impatient** to start reading it and I suspect I'll be rather **antisocial** for a while!

Test 35

Step 1:

Word	'-ant'	'-ance'
observe	observant	observance
hesitate	hesitant	hesitance
tolerate	tolerant	tolerance

Step 2:

There has been an alarming **<u>frequency</u> / frequancy** of accidents outside our local supermarket.

Despite the fact that his hands were covered in red paint, Blake protested his **innocance / <u>innocence</u>**.

"If you can't make it, at least have the **<u>decency</u> / decancy** to let me know!" complained Markus.

Step 3:

Word	'-ant'	'-ance'	'-ent'	'-ence'
assist	assistant	assistance		
obey			obedient	obedience
differ			different	difference
insist			insistent	insistence
comply	compliant	compliance		
coincide			coincident	coincidence

Test 36

Step 1:

<u>dependable</u> / dependible   <u>incredible</u> / incredable

<u>comfortable</u> / comfortible   <u>reasonable</u> / reasonible

<u>enjoyable</u> / enjoyible   horrable / <u>horrible</u>

Step 2:

Adjective	Adverb
considerable	considerably
tolerable	tolerably
adorable	adorably
demonstrable	demonstrably

Step 3:

forcible; changeable; noticeable; reliable; recognisable; visible

Test 37

Step 1:

i(s)land   (h)onourable   colum(n)

dou(b)tful   recei(p)t   (h)our

(k)nuckles   (p)sychologist

We(d)nesday   cas(t)le

Step 2:

knock   government   parliament   calf   **h**eir

com**b**   listen   bustle   salmon   reco**g**nise

Step 3:

1. island   2. scenery   3. folk   4. yacht   5. half   6. knew

Test 38

Step 1:

receive, ceiling, conceive, deceit, perceive

receipt, height, beige, eight

Step 2:

science, shriek, weird, glacier, conceited

Step 3:

protein; niece; seize; caffeine; siege

Test 39

Step 1:

aisle – isle   seen – scene   threw – through

quite – quiet   effect – affect   advice – advise

Step 2:

We **wondered** if we should **proceed** with **our** plan to go to the **beach** as it was **pouring** down. However, it wasn't long before the **fair weather** returned.

Step 3:

Accept any suitable sentences containing the words used in the correct context.

Test 40: Progress Test 4

Step 1:

Shona mixed the **substence / <u>substance</u>** in the beaker.

We held a one-minute silence in **<u>remembrance</u> / rememberence** of those who died.

inconceivable; **dis**regard; **im**material; **il**legible

<u>It is with regret that I have to inform you that Mr Williams will retire effective next month.</u>

Step 2:

<u>dismal</u>   furious   <u>bleak</u>   upset   annoying

grateful   brave   <u>inquisitive</u>   <u>unconcerned</u>   reserved

lov**able**; flex**ible**; resist**ible**; desir**able**

Step 3:

alter – altar   whale – wail   aloud – allowed

device – devise   desert – dessert   stationery – stationary

I demand Mr Robinson **be** present at the council committee meeting this evening.